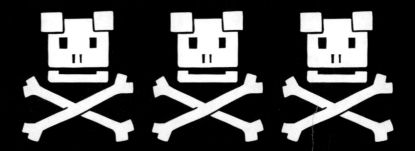

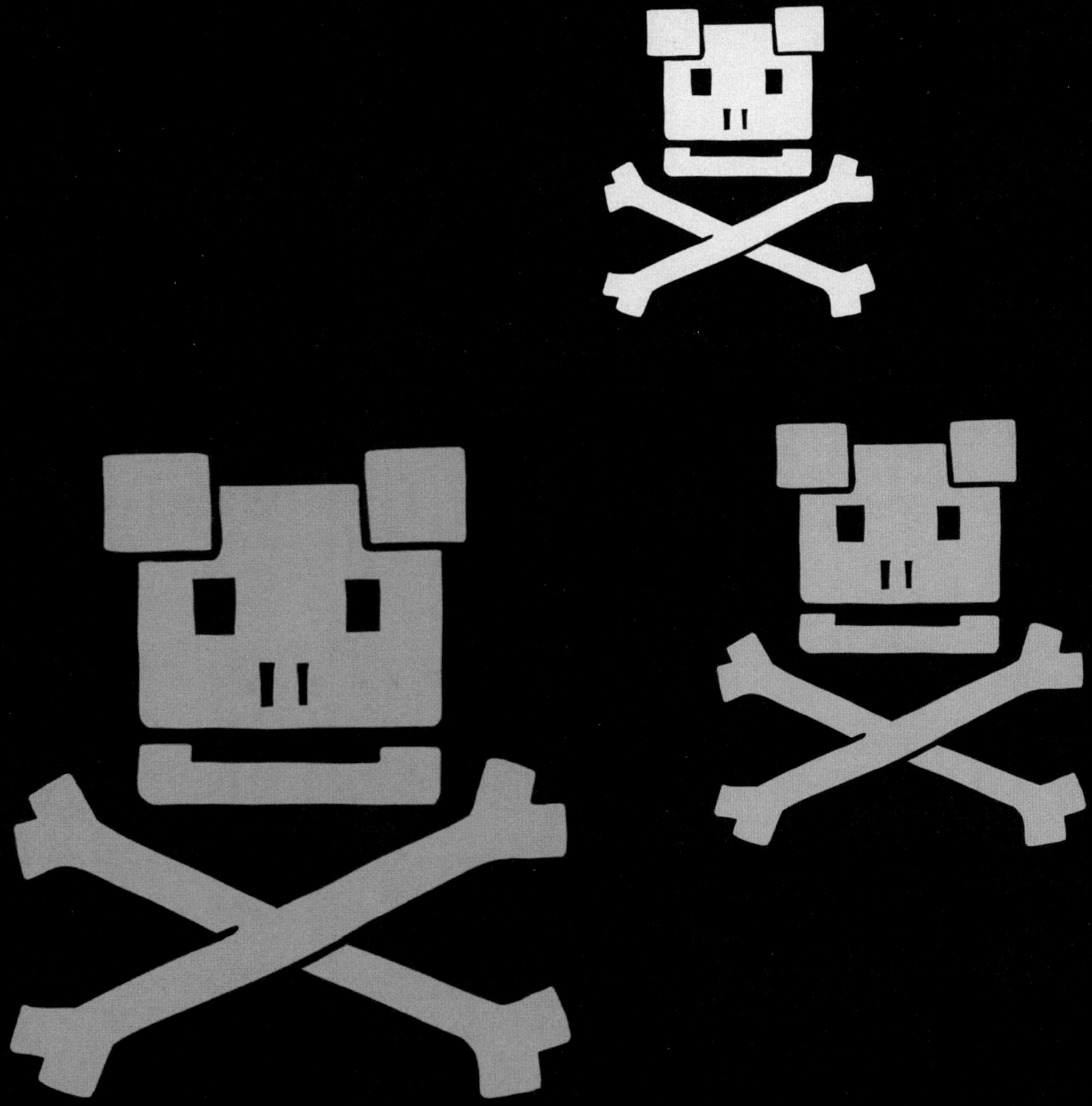

THREE LITTLE HACKERS

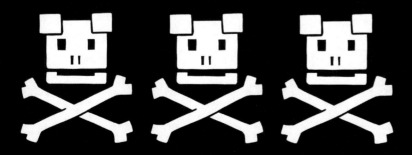

THREE LITTLE
HACKERS

Written and Illustrated by
Marcus J. Carey

This book is dedicated to my wife, children, and grandkids.

You all continue to inspire me.

I love you all.

-MJC

Once upon a time, there were three little hackers. Alice, Bob, and Charlie were all computer masters.

Their parents were white hat hackers, no kidding!

White hat hackers catch bad guys on the internet for a living.

Their parents gave them computers for their birthday,
but they came with a few rules that the little hackers must obey.

Do your homework first, especially you brothers.

If you need help coding you can ask your mother.

Have fun online but privacy is a must.
There are wolves in sheep's clothing that you should not trust!

Charlie liked to play games with castles and dragons,
but one of the other players kept on nagging.

The person asked, "Do you live by the park, library, or school?"
Charlie replied, "No silly goose, I live by the pool!"

At that moment Charlie's face turned bright red, because he remembered what his parents had said.

When strangers ask questions, you don't know their motivation, they can put pieces of information together to find your location.

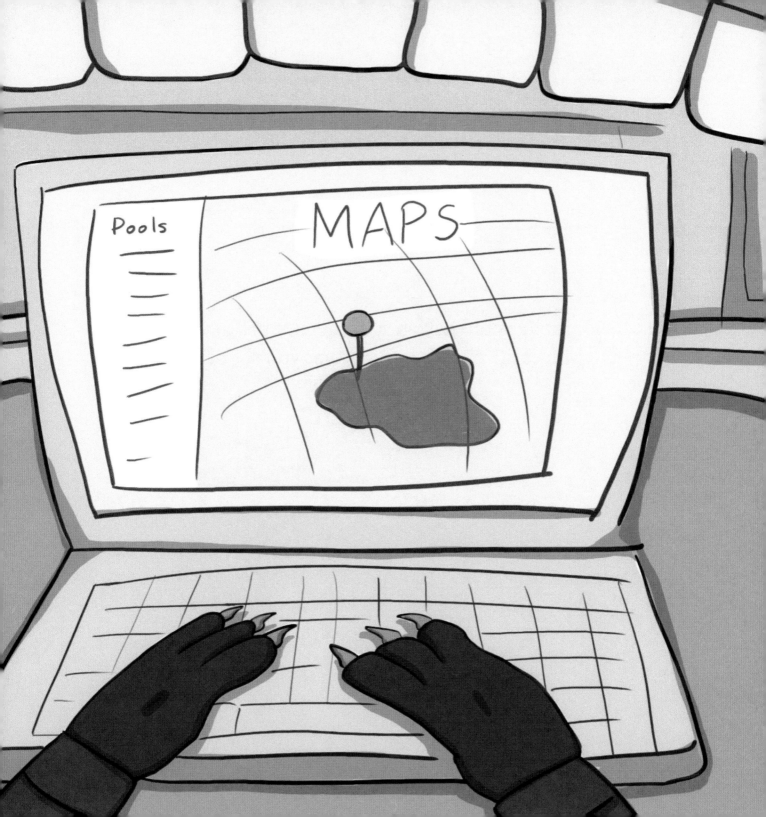

Charlie forgot he could have fun online but privacy is a must.
There are wolves in sheep's clothing that you should not trust!

The wolf said,

"The more secrets they give, the easier they are to find.
I will track them down and I promise I won't be kind!"

Bob loves chess, checkers, and games of strategy,
but one of Bob's opponents was very, very chatty.

They asked, "What college do you go to? Surely you can tell."
Bob laughed and typed back, "That's funny, I'm only twelve."

Strangers will say anything online, but don't believe, because bad guys will say anything to decieve.

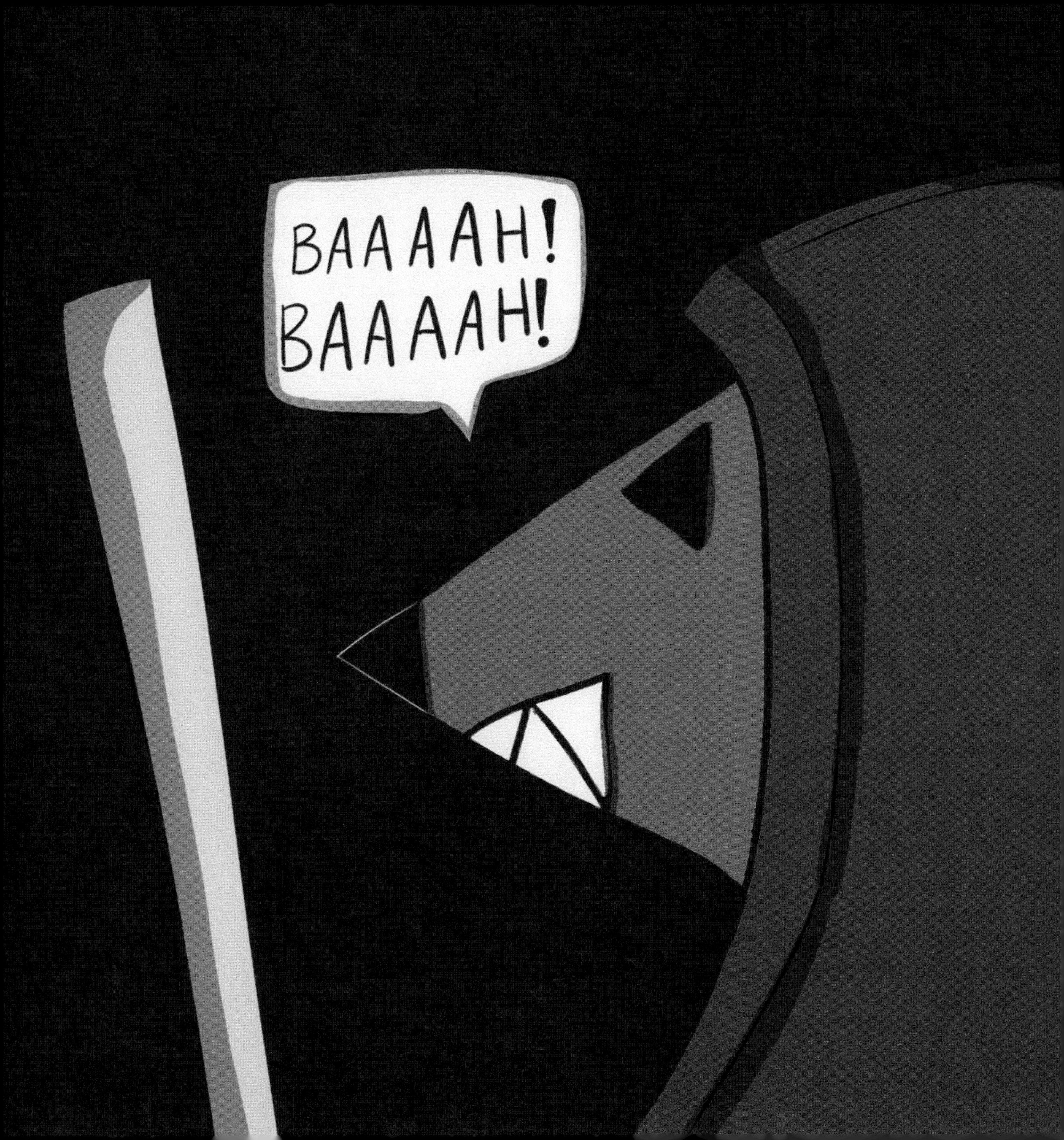
BAAAAH! BAAAAH!

Bob forgot he could have fun online but privacy is a must.
There are wolves in sheep's clothing you should not trust!

The wolf laughed and said,

"The more information they give me the easier they are to find,
I will track them down, and I promise I won't be kind!"

Alice loved playing action and adventure games online, but there was one teammate that was creepy all the time.

They said, "What's your address? I promise you no harm."
Alice thought about it for a second and it set off an alarm.

Alice remembered she could have fun online but privacy is a must.
There are wolves in sheep's clothing that you should not trust!

So Alice told her parents and it was such a big relief,
the wolf did not know that the parents contacted the police.

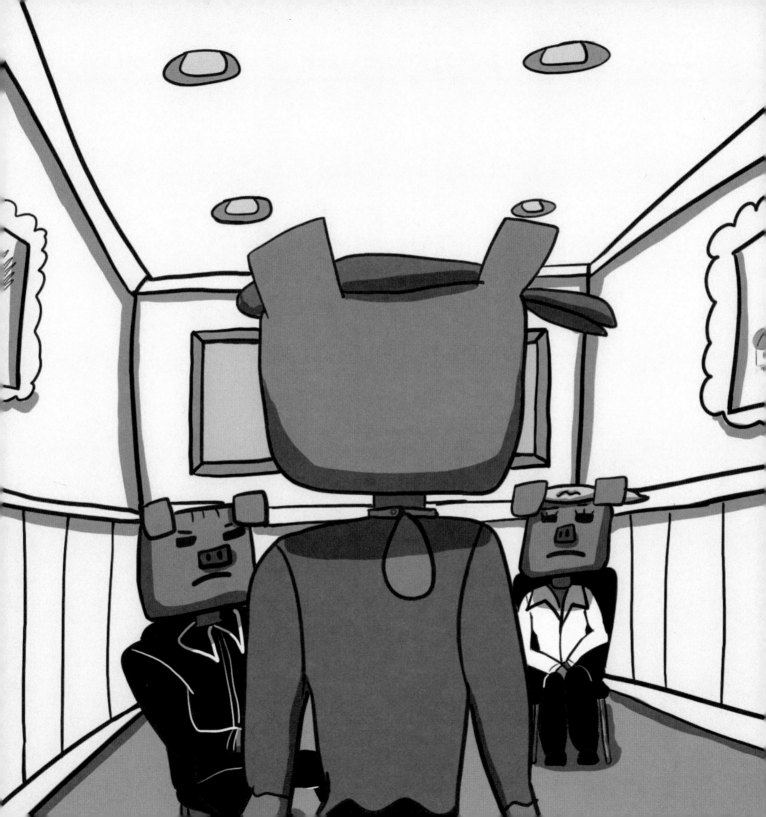

So the parents and police decided to set a trap,
they fooled the wolf by sending him a location on a map.

Then the wolf showed up at that exact address.

The police surprised the wolf and said, "You're under arrest!"

When a stranger asks for your secrets say "No way!"
They may track you down when your parents are away.

Remember you can have fun online but privacy is a must,
there are wolves in sheep's clothing that you should not trust.

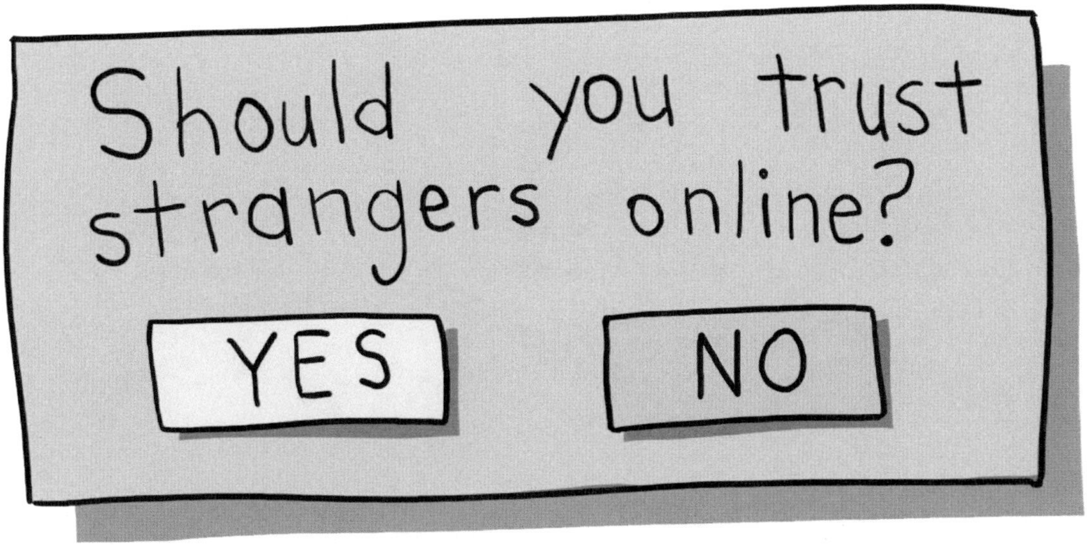
Should you trust strangers online?
YES
NO

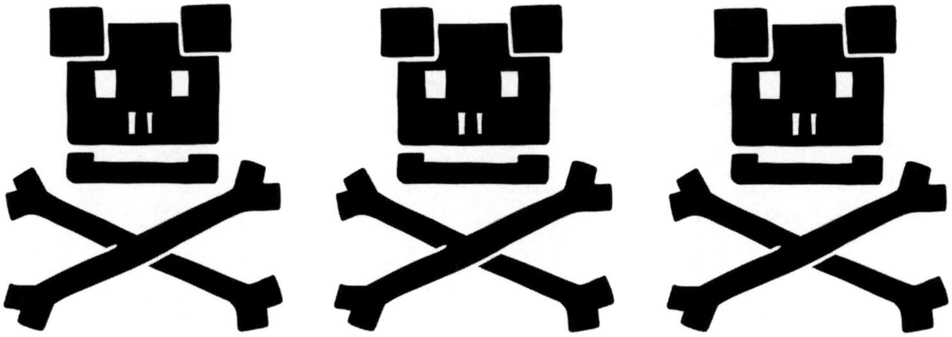

Made in the USA
Monee, IL
09 August 2020